HORSES
Photo-Fact Collection

W9-ABP-603

Scientific Consultant
Jennifer Gresham
Director of Education
Zoo New England

Kidsbooks®

Copyright © 2012 Kidsbooks, LLC
3535 West Peterson Avenue
Chicago, IL 60659

Printed in China
011201001SZ

Visit us at www.kidsbooks.com®

Quarter horse

CONTENTS

Horse Story

Herd-dwelling animals, horses live in large groups with clearly defined social relationships. As social animals, horses were domesticated by humans over 5,000 years ago and continue to help people today. Horses have special adaptations that make them important to people, and enable them to live in a variety of places. Some horses still live on their own, without people, and can be found all over the globe.

Quarter horses

Thoroughbred horse

Ready to Ride

What is the only animal that can run for miles and leap over fences carrying a rider on its back? A horse, of course. Over the centuries horses have helped humans more than any other animal.

Pony Vs Horse

Ponies are technically horses, but they are much smaller and have a different character. The Shetland is the smallest pony, measuring four feet to the shoulder. The tallest horse, the Shire horse, can be more than six feet in height.

Appaloosa horse

Shire horse

Shetland pony

The Horse Family

The Equidae family consists of horses, zebras, and donkeys. Though they are not a type of horse, zebras and horses share many similarities: they both have hard hooves, live and graze in herds, and have similar body shapes.

Common zebra

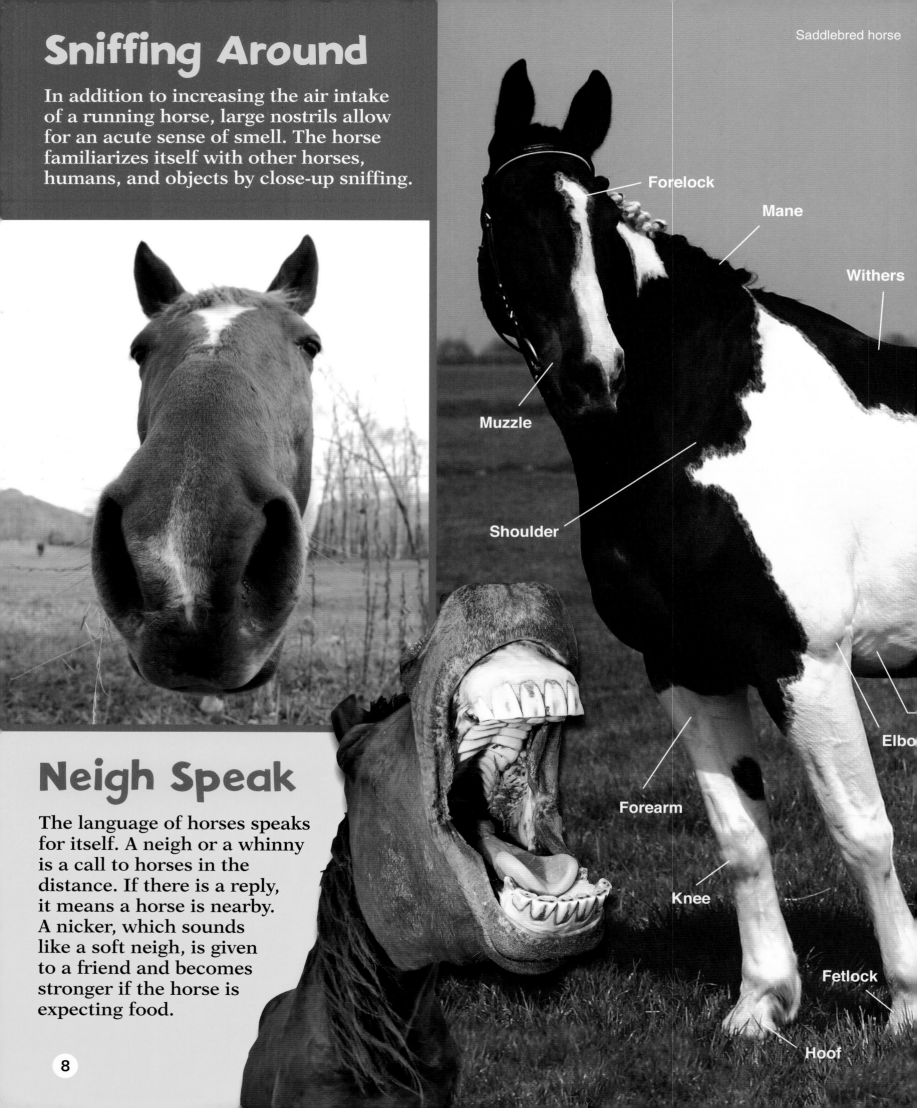

Sniffing Around

In addition to increasing the air intake of a running horse, large nostrils allow for an acute sense of smell. The horse familiarizes itself with other horses, humans, and objects by close-up sniffing.

Neigh Speak

The language of horses speaks for itself. A neigh or a whinny is a call to horses in the distance. If there is a reply, it means a horse is nearby. A nicker, which sounds like a soft neigh, is given to a friend and becomes stronger if the horse is expecting food.

Saddlebred horse

Forelock

Mane

Withers

Muzzle

Shoulder

Forearm

Knee

Elbo

Fetlock

Hoof

Fine Features

A horse has many remarkable traits, including panoramic vision, the ability to convey emotion, and the ability to sleep standing up. Because horses have all these specialized features, humans needed to develop an extensive set of equine-related vocabulary. From the bristly tail to the soft muzzle, every section of a horse has a unique name.

Loins

Croup

Tail

Belly

Stifle

Barrel

Hock

Cannon bone

Hear That?

With ears that swivel like antennas, a horse can pick up sounds from all directions. The position of a horse's ears also indicates mood. If the ears point back, the horse is angry or frightened; if one ear is pointing back and the other forward, the horse is uncertain.

Draft horse

Pony Tales

Although they look similar, ponies are different from horses. Ponies are more petite than horses, usually growing no higher than 58 inches—yet they are sturdier on their feet than the horse. The wild moorlands of the British Isles have produced several breeds of ponies. One of them, the Dartmoor, has been bred with other horses so there are few purebred Dartmoor ponies today.

Miniature Horses

Miniature horses are not ponies. This distinctive breed of horse averages 30 inches in height to the shoulder. Known to be good-tempered and friendly, miniature horses have also been bred as pets and service animals.

Hardy Horse

Considered to be one of the oldest native breeds, the British Exmoor pony is well suited for hardy environments with its hairy, hooded eyes. It is also very independent and still semi-wild, as many are not domesticated.

Pure Pony

Though it is called a horse, the small Icelandic horse is really a pony. It has not been crossbred with any other horses for more than 1,000 years—making it the purest pony breed in existence.

First Steps

Like humans, baby horses, or foals, develop gradually and with the loving care of a mother. Once a foal is born, it tries to stand on its wobbly legs within the first hour. From there, it begins nursing and receiving care from its mother. After a few weeks, a foal will graze with other horses in the fields, and it will continue to nurse for about a year after being born.

American Quarter horse

Nap Time

A foal, like all babies, needs plenty of rest. It will frequently lie down and nap. At the first sign of danger, a foal quickly gets to its feet and runs to its mother's side.

Thoroughbred horses

The Folks

An adult female horse is called a mare, and an adult male horse is called a stallion. Mares reach adulthood between their first and second years. Mares and stallions mate during the spring—a time when, in the wild, food is more plentiful.

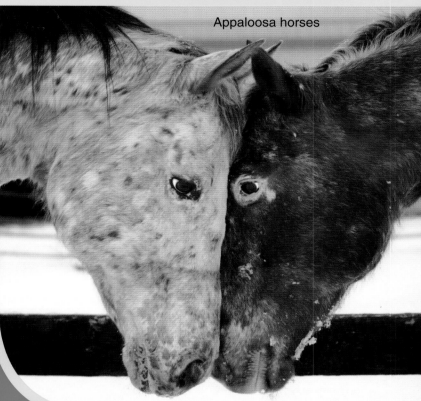

Appaloosa horses

Foaling Around

A female foal is called a filly; a male foal is called a colt. As they grow, colts and fillies love to play. They nip one another and kick up their legs. Running together teaches foals about survival behavior.

Falabella horses

Paint horse

Hot & COLD

Crossing a hotblood with a coldblood produces a warmblood. These horses are popular in competitive events because they embody characteristics of both hotbloods and coldbloods: speed and strength, respectively.

Chill Out!

Many coldbloods are large, heavy horses from cold climates. Strength, rather than speed, is the hallmark of a coldblood. The biggest breed of horse in the world, the coldblooded British Shire horse, reaches 6 feet at the shoulder and weighs up to 2,900 pounds.

British Shire horse

Sizing Them Up

Horses are divided into three groups that indicate where the breed originated. The three types are the hotbloods, the coldbloods, and the warmbloods. Some horses are from hot and humid environments. Others hail from lands with freezing temperatures. And horses in the last category, warmbloods, result from crossbreeding hotbloods and coldbloods. The Arabian horse, a hotblood, originated in desert–like conditions where grazing lands were poor.

Color Coating

Horses come in a variety of colors. One of the most beautiful horse colors is palomino, which describes a gold coat with a white mane and tail. Unlike most horses, which are classified by breed, Palominos are cross-registered for their breed and color.

Horses in Time

Of all domesticated animals, the horse was the last to be tamed by humans. Before they were ever ridden, horses and donkeys were trained to pull carts and chariots. The ancient Greeks and Romans used horses for chariot racing, which was first staged at the Olympic Games in 680 B.C.

The Trojan Horse

According to legend, the Greeks built an enormous wooden horse and left it as a "gift" outside the city walls of Troy. When the horse was brought inside, Greek soldiers hidden in the horse's hollow belly leapt out and conquered the city.

Shire horse

War Horses

For 5,000 years, up to World War I, humans used horses to assist them in wars. Riding without saddles, ancient warriors battled their enemies. In the Middle Ages, knights rode into battle on horses that were as heavily armored as they were.

Picture Perfect

Early people hunted horses for food and their sturdy hide. Scientists have found early cave drawings depicting scenes of ancient people riding and hunting on horses.

To America

About 8,000 years ago, horses became extinct in North America. No one knows why. It was not until the 16th century, when Spanish conquerors arrived in Mexico, that horses were reintroduced to the Americas. Beginning in the 18th century, carts and coaches harnessed to horses rattled along dirt roads of early America, moving people and goods from one place to another. Horses simpified hunting and moving camp.

Quarter horses

Cattle Drive

Starting in the 1860s, cattle from Texas ranches were herded over vast distances to supply growing cities with fresh beef. The teams of cowboys who did this work were completely dependent on their horses, mostly wild mustangs.

WESTWARD HO!

In the mid-19th century, thousands of Americans headed west seeking more land and better lives. Wagon trains, pulled by horses or mules, made the trek across the plains and over the Rocky Mountains. The trip took months, and many settlers and horses did not survive the hardships.

Mules

ST. JOSEPH

SACRAMENTO

1860-1861 PONY EXPRESS 4c

UNITED STATES POSTAGE

Going Postal

From April 1860 to October 1861, mail was carried across the United States by horseback. It took ten days by Pony Express for a letter to reach California from the Midwest. Each Pony Express rider covered 60 miles at a stretch, stopping to change horses about every 10 miles.

Show and Sport

Organized races on horseback were popular with the ancient Greeks and Romans. Called "the sport of kings," horse racing now takes place at famous courses around the world. The steeplechase, a more dramatic form of horse racing, began in 18th-century England. The goal was to reach a distant landmark—usually a church steeple—by galloping across open fields and leaping over fences and hedges along the way.

Let's Dance

Classical riding is a competitive system of horse training that dates back hundreds of years. The most difficult movements include one in which the horse trots in place with high, springy steps, and one where the horse spins in a tiny circle, its hind legs staying almost on the same spot.

Thoroughbred horse

Arabian horse

Desert Games

One of the world's most spectacular horse festivals, called fantasia, takes place in Morocco. In a fantasia, a line of riders charge straight ahead until a signal is given by the leader. Then the riders stand up in their stirrups, bring their horses to an abrupt stop, and fire rifles into the air.

Barb horses

Horse Hockey

Polo is one of the fastest games in the world. Riding at full gallop, two teams, each with four riders, use bamboo mallets to hit a ball through a goal post.

Quarter horses and Thoroughbred horses

Donkey Work

With little nourishment, donkeys are able to carry heavy loads over long distances. Strong and surefooted, they have been used as pack and riding animals for thousands of years.

Australia **27c**

1891 Shand Mason Steam Fire Engine

Fire Fighters

Think of it—in the days before fire trucks, three large horses pulled fire engines. Once the alarm sounded, harnesses slid onto the horses' backs from overhead frames, firemen fastened them up, and the entire rig was ready to roll in three to five minutes.

Working 9 to 5

Today we usually do not see many horses in the cities where we live. Nowadays, people may take nostalgic horse-drawn carriage trips around town. But before there were cars or buses, light draft horses, such as the Welsh Cob and the Cleveland Bay, were harnessed to carriages that carried people around the city. Coldblooded breeds like the Clydesdale were used to haul everything from milk carts to barrels of beer.

Draft horses

Belgian horse

Farm Horses

From about A.D. 500, when the Chinese invented the rigid horse collar, until the invention of the tractor, horses were used for all kinds of farm work. In some parts of the world, they still work on farms. Horse-drawn plowing competitions remain popular in Europe and the U.S.

How Wild is Wild?

Sadly, there are very few truly wild horses—horses that have never been domesticated by humans—living in the world today. Loss of habitat has taken its toll. Some horses we call "wild" are more correctly called "feral." This means that they are descended from domesticated stock but are no longer under human control.

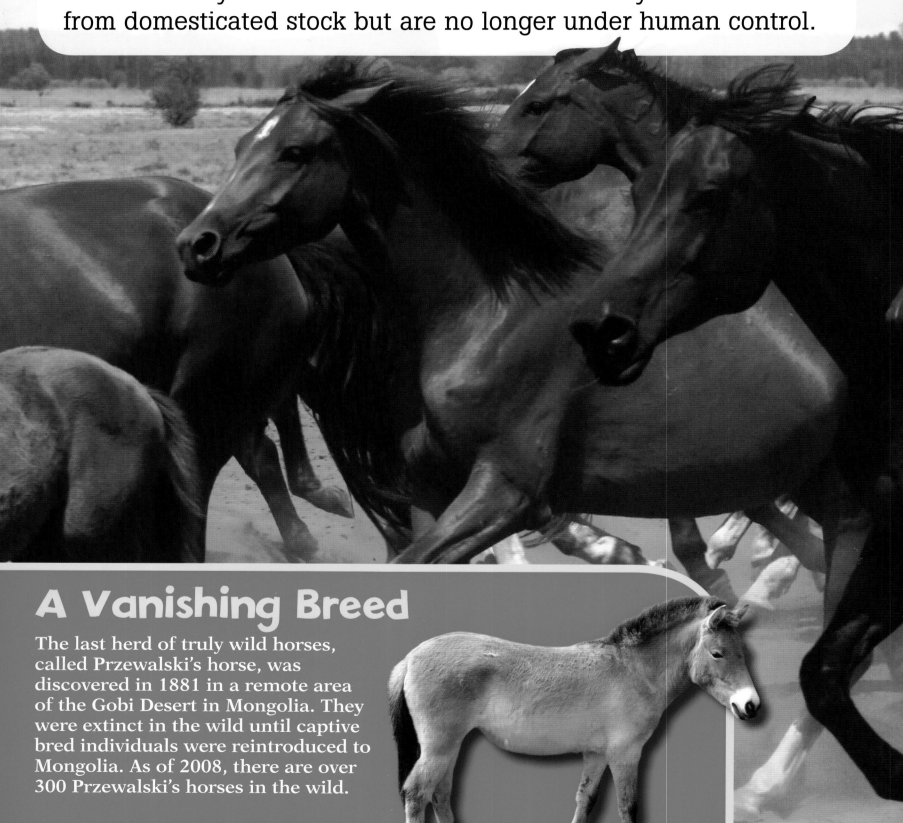

A Vanishing Breed

The last herd of truly wild horses, called Przewalski's horse, was discovered in 1881 in a remote area of the Gobi Desert in Mongolia. They were extinct in the wild until captive bred individuals were reintroduced to Mongolia. As of 2008, there are over 300 Przewalski's horses in the wild.

Morgan horses

Chincoteague pony

Swimming Ponies

Some wild horses are known for their affinity for water. Chincoteague ponies, native to the cost of Virginia, and Camargue horses from southern France live in marshy areas. Chincoteagues even swim across small channels.

WILD MUSTANGS

More than 400 years ago, the Spanish brought horses to North America. Some of those strong, fast-running Spanish horses escaped, multiplied, and formed the Mustang herds that still roam remote parts of the American West. Once hunted almost to extinction, Mustangs are now protected by law.

Horses Today

Although we do not rely on horses as much as we did before the invention of the motor, but horses are still an essential part of modern life. Horses and ponies are used in many countries to farm and to carry loads, and they have been part of parades and pageantry for centuries. Some horses are also used in rodeos, competitions which test skills developed by cowboys in the early days of cattle ranching.

Giddy Up!

Mounted police are found in cities throughout the world. Their job is to patrol crowds, parks, and public spaces.

Quarter horse

Quarter horse

Mules

Trekking

Horses, ponies, and mules are used in treks through the wilderness, helping people visit remote areas inaccessible by car. It would be impossible for a human to carry supplies to the bottom of the Grand Canyon.

KENTUCKY HORSE PARK

The state of Kentucky is famous for its horses and pays tribute to them at the Kentucky Horse Park. More than 40 different horse and pony breeds, including some world class champions, can be seen in the park's stables.

Thoroughbred horses

The Human Touch

Most horses and ponies today are raised by humans. They are accustomed to handling and the routines of a stable. They have the ability to adapt to human ways. If properly treated and cared for, a horse will form a close and affectionate bond with its human handler. Grooming also builds a close bond between horse and human.

Quarter horse

Thoroughbred horse

Break a Horse

A horse is trained by using various methods to curb its natural tendency to take flight. Training a horse to accept a halter, a bridle, and eventually a rider, is a slow process that requires patience and sensitivity.

Quarter horse

New Shoes

Every six to eight weeks a stabled horse must be fitted for new metal shoes. This is not because the old shoes are worn out, but because the hard outer wall of a horse's hooves grows so fast.

MUNCHieS

Stabled horses are fed hay and grains at regular meal times, and must have fresh water before each feeding. Horses also like the taste of salt and sweets, especially apples.

GLOSSARY

Breaking a horse: To train a horse to submit to a human's wishes.

Cannon bone: The lower leg bone of a horse.

Classical riding: A competitive system of horse training.

Coldbloods: A term used to describe large, heavy horses from cold climates; e.g., British Shire.

Colt: A male foal.

Draft horse: A horse used to pull carriages and haul heavy materials; used extensively before motorized vehicles were available.

Equidae family: The animal family that horses belong in, which consists of horses, zebras, and asses.

Feral: Wild horses descended from domesticated stock, but not under human control.

Fetlock: The part of a horse's leg that corresponds to a human's ankle.

Filly: A female foal.

Foal: A baby horse.

Forelock: A lock of hair growing from the front of a horse's head.

Hock: The joint on the hind leg of a horse that corresponds to a human's ankle.

Hotbloods: A term used to describe light and fast horses, e.g., Arabians and Barbs, from a warm climate.

Mane: Long, heavy hair growing about the head and neck of a horse.

Mare: An adult female horse.

Miniature horse: A distinct breed of horse, not to be confused with a pony. It grows to about 30 inches in height to the shoulder.

Mustang: A small, wild horse of the western plains brought to North America from Spain.

Muzzle: The area that includes a horse's nose, lips, and mouth.

Neigh: The sound a horse makes when calling to another horse; also called a whinny.

Nicker: A soft neigh.

Polo: Game played on horseback; riders use mallets to hit a ball through a goal.

Pony: A small horse that is no taller than 56.8 inches (14.2 hands) to the shoulder.

Rodeo: An event that tests the skills of cowboys, including calf roping and saddle bronco riding.

Shetland: The smallest pony, measuring four feet to the shoulder.

Shire: The tallest horse, measuring more than six feet in height.

Stallion: An adult male horse.

Steeplechase: Dramatic form of horse racing that involves riders galloping across fields and leaping over obstacles to reach a landmark.

Stifle: The joint above the hock in the hind leg that corresponds to the human knee.

Thoroughbred: A breed of horse bred from an Arabian and a Barb.

Trojan horse: Hollow, wooden horse of Greek legend, filled with soldiers to conquer the city of Troy.

Warmblood: A cross between a coldblood and a hotblood; e.g. Paint horse.

Whinny: The sound a horse makes when calling to another horse; also called a neigh.

Wild Mustang: Wild horses brought from Spain to North America.

Withers: The part of a horse's anatomy just above the top of the shoulder blades.